FAMILY TALK
with
James C. Dobson

dads and daughters

Practical Advice and Encouragement for Men Shaping the Next Generation of Women

DR. JAMES DOBSON

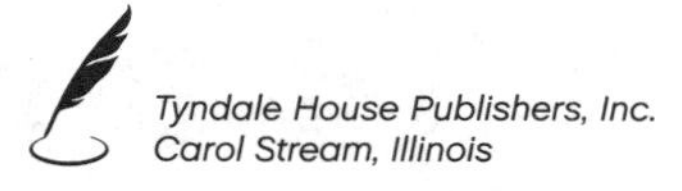

Tyndale House Publishers, Inc.
Carol Stream, Illinois

Visit Tyndale's exciting Web site at www.tyndale.com.

TYNDALE and Tyndale's quill logo are registered trademarks of Tyndale House Publishers, Inc.

Dads and Daughters: Practical Advice and Encouragement for Men Shaping the Next Generation of Women

Adapted from *Bringing Up Girls* first published in 2010 by Tyndale House Publishers, Inc.

Designed by Stephen Vosloo

Library of Congress Cataloging-in-Publication Data

Dobson, James C., date.
Dads and daughters / James Dobson.
p. cm.
Includes bibliographical references (p.).
ISBN 978-1-4143-5463-7 (sc)
1. Fathers—Religious life. 2. Fathers and daughters—Religious aspects—Christianity. I. Title.
BV4529.17.D62 2011
248.8'45—dc22 2010047574

Printed in the United States of America

17 16 15 14 13 12 11
7 6 5 4 3 2

1

Introduction

IT IS MY PRIVILEGE to share some thoughts and findings with you in this booklet, which is the first in a series of small publications devoted to the well-being of families. The content was excerpted from my book, *Bringing Up Girls*, and begins with this dedication.

> The passion I feel for the subject at hand is related to the daughter who still calls me Dad. She is grown now, but I love her like I did when we were first introduced in the delivery room. Something electric occurred

between us on that mystical night,
and it endures today.

Those words were written to my beloved daughter, Danae, who is a source of great joy and pride for her mother and me. Our relationship is the springboard for one of the major themes of *Bringing Up Girls*, which focuses on dads and their daughters. We will examine this relationship and explain why it is so vitally important to girls. It comes down to this: a wise and dedicated father holds the keys to his daughter's feminine identity, her sense of self-worth, and her future relationship with boys and men. Indeed, his affirmation, or the lack thereof, will play a role in every aspect of her life, even influencing her choice of a marital partner. I am saddened to report that all too often, a dad fails to understand his daughter's complex nature and misses the opportunities that are presented to him.

Let's consider first how family dynamics tend to play out at home and explore why daughters often draw the short straw. A dad's first obligation is to meet the emotional needs of his wife. He may not fully understand her, but he knows she is different from him in ways that require his attention and involvement.

Second, fathers have a major responsibility to meet the needs of their sons. It is is their job to teach them to be men and to understand the meaning of masculinity. Mothers are not equipped to accomplish that important objective. Dads may not be willing to accept that responsibility, but they know they should.

That brings us to the position girls usually hold in the family. Pay attention now, because I am about to tell you something that I consider to be of prime importance: *daughters tend to be third in line for the attention of the man of the family*. I have drawn that conclusion after many years of working with families. I'll say it again for emphasis: fathers know intuitively that their boys require special attention, discipline, and leadership, but they are often unaware of how urgently their daughters also need them. Some dads apparently see this yearning for affirmation among their girls as the exclusive responsibility of mothers. Raising daughters is seen as "women's work." Thus, the girls are often overlooked or largely ignored. It is my firm conviction, however, that girls need their dads as much as boys do, and in some cases, even more.

This will be a new idea for some men, but careful research bears it out. Furthermore, when girls are deprived of the needed affirmation, an inner longing occurs that may continue for the rest of their lives. Only women who have experienced this emptiness can relate to what I am describing.

Let me illustrate that yearning and how it was expressed by a woman who crossed my path briefly. On Father's Day a few years ago, I asked our radio listeners to call our studios and to record a message specifically for their dads. More than six hundred people participated, most of them women. I listened to some of the recordings, and we aired them on Father's Day. Not one of these messages focused on what the father had done professionally. None of the callers said, "Thanks, Dad, for earning a lot of money" or "Thanks for the big house you provided for us" or "Thanks for the Cadillac [or Mercedes or

BMW]." No one mentioned living in an upscale neighborhood.

Instead, caller after caller said, "Thanks, Dad, for loving me and for being there for me." Some said with strong emotion, "Thank you for letting me interrupt you, even when you were busy." Nearly all of the calls coming from women mentioned the presence of tenderness in the relationship.

We kept a transcript of those recordings, and there is one that I wish everyone could hear. These are the actual words expressed sorrowfully by a woman, perhaps in her late thirties:

> Hi, this is Kathy from Georgia, with a letter for my daddy. I don't know where things went wrong, when the pain, prescriptions, and alcohol began. I was just a kid. You tried to never let me down, Daddy, but many times you did. Daddy, in 1978, always and still, I was thinking of you as Father's Day approached. I searched for just the right card for you, my darling daddy,

> and mailed it late. But Daddy, all day long your phone was busy. You died alone on the floor, beside your upturned phone, on Father's Day. When I got to Portland, my card was still in your mailbox. You never knew, Daddy. I was too late. God, help me always remember that late is better than never, but it's not good enough. Daddy, you died without experiencing my care and my love on Father's Day.

Kathy's words still echo in my mind today: "Daddy . . . ," she said, "always and still, I was thinking of you." Even though decades had passed since the painful experiences of her childhood, this woman continued to grieve for her absentee father. The recording reveals no anger or resentment in her voice—just lingering sorrow because her "darling daddy" was never there for her. I can't tell you how many grown women have told me similar stories about their fathers who disappointed them again and again.

To illustrate the point further, we'll turn

now to conversations I have had with college women, who expressed the same sentiment. You will find their comments insightful—and at times deeply moving.

2

Young Women Talk about Their Fathers

EARLY IN THE THREE-YEAR PROCESS of writing *Bringing Up Girls*, I invited forty very intelligent, academically gifted college and university women to join me for a discussion about this topic. At the time, they were attending a semester-long Christian educational experience called the Focus Leadership Institute.[1] We served them lunch and then I explained what I was writing. I asked these young ladies for advice on what they thought should be included in my book.

The comments made during this spontaneous discussion were recorded and then subsequently transcribed. Though the students were invited to talk about any related subject of their choosing, our conversations moved in a straight line to their relationships with their fathers. As you will see, most of them acknowledged that something vital was missing there. Others were grateful for what their dads had done to make them feel valuable and respected. Almost all of them spoke of the need for greater emotional connection with their dads.

I hope fathers will not be defensive about what was said by these remarkable young women but, instead, will hear within their comments "the language of their hearts." I began by thanking them for participating and made this introductory comment:

> I have talked to many college-age women in the process of writing *Bringing Up Girls*, and I can summarize the most frequent comment I have heard like this: "My father is a good man. He has worked hard to earn a living for our family, and he's been faithful to my mother

[others said just the opposite]. Still, I never felt that he really admired or wanted to be close to me. He was very, very busy doing what he did, but he didn't have time for me. I felt like I was just there around the house, but he often didn't even seem to notice me."

Was this something that others of you have also experienced?

These were the reactions of the young women on that day.

Girl #1: What you just said, Dr. Dobson, describes exactly what I feel. And I've heard it from so many of my friends. In fact, our greatest uneasiness about getting married is the fear that our future husbands will not be affirming and caring.

Girl #2: It is essential that girls get affirmation from their fathers, because that's something I didn't experience growing up. That is the foundation of all my insecurities—the feeling that I wasn't really loved by my father. It is the root of everything I'm dealing with.

Girl #3: That hits home with me, too. My dad was a good father, but he would compare me to girls in the media and complain that I didn't look like them. He told me I didn't work out enough, and he also called attention to what I was eating. He would say, "Do you realize where that's gonna go? That's gonna go right to your hips or to your legs." And so . . . I wasn't a full-fledged anorexic, I guess, but I worked out all the time. I was also dieting, and it got to the point where I wouldn't eat anything.

For the longest time I said that I had forgiven my dad, but it affected my relationship with Christ and made me question what it meant to have a heavenly Father who loved me. Fortunately, there are other men in my life who have supported and affirmed me, including my two brothers. But in the past six months, my dad has really worked hard at mending our relationship.

JCD: Did you ever sit down and tell your father how you feel?

Girl #3: Yes, sir. And he actually wrote a letter to me since I came to the Institute about a month ago. He said how sorry he was that he didn't realize what a negative impact his comments had on me. So it's been really good, and I think the only reason I can actually forgive him now is because I have acknowledged Christ as my heavenly Father.

Girl #4: When I was going from a child to a woman—experiencing puberty—my dad just totally stepped back from me. It was as though he no longer knew how to relate to me. But it was a time when I desperately needed him in my life.

JCD: Have you ever asked him

why he wasn't there for you at that time?

Girl #4: No. I don't have a good relationship with my father at all. It has led me to get involved in some dangerous behavior.

JCD: Did he spend time with you when you were a child?

Girl #4: No, and even when he did, it was completely on his terms. He was very involved in his profession, so on his day off he had things he wanted to do. He invited me to join him, but his idea of a good time was to shoot firearms. So even at four years old, I was already shooting guns. It wasn't anything that I ever really enjoyed, but it was the only way to get affirmation from my father on any level. He would introduce me to people by saying, "This is my daughter. She just shot eighteen out of twenty on the skeet field an hour ago." He never told them about any of my other abilities.

JCD: He never affirmed your femininity?

Girl #4: No, it was always about guns. I finally just backed away from him.

JCD: Is it too late to connect with your dad?

Girl #4: I don't know. I think God's working on it, but there's a lot of abuse in that relationship too. So . . . I think it's one of those things.

Girl #5: Hearing these heart-breaking stories today makes me thankful that I have a loving and affirming father, but he was not perfect. He was very sarcastic at home, and he joked around a lot. I've never, ever in my life been a skinny child. I'm built like my dad. My sisters and I would wear tank tops and shorts to bed, and in the morning when we came down to breakfast, my dad would pinch my side and make a joke about my weight. He never intended to be mean, but he would talk before he thought and say things that really hurt me.

Girl #6: My father was not like that. He told my sister and me that it was the inner beauty that mattered. He would also tell us how beautiful we were on the outside. And so that's what got me through junior high and high school, because I dealt with self-esteem issues. I'll never forget in sixth grade, having people ask me, "Why don't you look like your sister?" I was a very late bloomer, but she was an early bloomer. So I had four years of extreme insecurity where people would say, "Why are you shorter, and why are you so skinny? What's wrong with you?" My dad got me through that. If it weren't for him, I don't know what I would have done.

Girl #7: You know, I'm just hearing these stories from many of you all [speaking to her classmates], and they make me so sad. I had no idea there were so many broken women in our group. And of course we all have different things that we are going through . . . but wow! I've just had such a different experience, and I realize that much of who I am is because of the affirmation I received growing up. One of the things that I love to hear is when my family says, "Oh, you look cute." That sounds so silly, but my dad told me that all the time, and it has just meant so much coming from my own father. I realize just how blessed I have been.

Girl #8: My father was a good man, but he was very passive, and I just wish he would have set a lot more boundaries and given me more critical input. That is what I missed most from him. Instead of worrying so much about hurting my feelings, I wish he had shown me that he had an opinion of what was right and wrong in my life. He was always trying to make sure that I was happy with our relationship, but I would rather that he would have been more forthright and said, "You know, I don't think this guy is right for you. This is what I see." I needed him to tell me that I mattered enough for him to guide me.

JCD: I have rarely heard a girl say, "I wish my dad had set more boundaries," but that desire is more common than people think. I believe many teens want their parents, and especially their fathers, to lead them. It is a way dads show they care.

I'm reminded of a single father who works here who told me something that happened when his daughter was ten or twelve, as I recall. They were watching television together one evening when a program came on that had some bad language and sexual themes in it. He didn't want to be a fuddy-duddy, so he simply went along with it. They watched the program a while longer, and finally he couldn't take it anymore. He turned off the set and said, "Honey, I just don't feel good about our watching this." His daughter said, "I thought you'd never turn it off, Dad." Adolescents need boundaries, even though they often act offended when limits are imposed.

Girl #9: I want to share something neat that my dad did for me. When I was probably seven or eight, we were driving to the beach on a vacation. I was in the back of the car and had my feet on the console between the front seats. My dad was driving, and we were at a stoplight when he reached back and touched my foot. He said, "You have the cutest feet." It meant a lot to me because I was a dancer, and sometimes my feet were not that nice, but to this day I love my feet. I love shoes. Just that simple compliment stayed with me. It was as though my dad selected that one feature to affirm. It still means so much to me. I'll never forget it.

JCD: Some people would consider what your dad did to have been an insignificant gesture, and yet you remember it vividly today. It illustrates just how important kindness and compliments are to children, and especially to girls. Conversely, even mild criticism or ridicule, especially about the physical body, can be very hurtful to a sensitive individual.

Girl #10: Just recently I received a Valentine's Day e-mail from my father. It was the first card or e-mail he has sent me since I was seven years old, and it meant the world to me. He was an alcoholic when I was young, but he has been recovering for the past two years. This is the first time in twenty-one years that he's gone more than two days without a drink.

JCD: That is a very touching story.

How many of the rest of you have ever received a Valentine card or e-mail from your father? [counting] That's about half. How many have been taken on a date by your father? [several raised their hands]

Girl #10: When I was seven, my dad would take me to breakfast on Saturday mornings, but there were always about five other men who came along. I was never with him one-on-one. I guess that was why I was always reaching for him. I chose to participate in sports that I thought my dad would be interested in. I love those activities now, but I think I chose them to try to connect with him in some way. I can't explain the love that I have for him, despite the pain that he has caused. I love him in a different way from anybody else on the face of this earth. It is indescribable and unconditional, and I can't explain why.

JCD: Even when a father consistently disappoints and hurts his daughter, he is still her dad and she will always crave his attention. She may be intensely angry at times and blame him for his failures as a dad, but there is usually something inside that longs for reconciliation with him. She is just made that way.

Girl #11: No matter how much your mom affirms you as a child, she can't compensate fully if something is missing in your relationship with your dad. Even if you have a full-time mom when you are growing up, you still need the validation of your dad. When he doesn't provide it, your entire life is affected and even the way you see things is different. That has happened to me.

Girl #12: My dad coached college football, which consumes all of a man's time. It is very difficult for a coach to have a healthy family, especially at the college level. I really didn't know my dad, but he was my hero. And that's what hurt, 'cause he wasn't just my hero; he was the hero of many thousands of kids around the state. He was an amazing man who made mistakes, and he paid for them gravely. In order to get my dad's attention, I would go to practice with him, and I wondered why he cared more for all those boys than he did about me.

I was the oldest, and he would tell me when he left for a game or for recruiting, "Take care of your mom." I was kind of like the dad of the family, even as a kid. And I felt like I wasn't a pretty enough girl. My mom is a very pretty lady, and men flocked to her. I never felt that way.

When dad was fired, he and my mom drifted even further apart, and they were soon divorced. I only heard them fighting once. They didn't speak much to each other. I just know my mother cried every day until the divorce was over. It really hurt me to watch her struggle. She lost her self-confidence, even though she was, and is, a very godly woman. [crying throughout the room]

My dad did a turnaround when he and my mom were divorced. He went through a time of depression for about four years after he was fired. And he worked his tail off to win back my sister and me, but I kept him at arm's length.

I quit telling either of my parents that I loved them. I decided that since I didn't tell my dad that I loved him, I just shouldn't tell my mom either, 'cause that wouldn't be fair. So I was like the kid who wouldn't let anybody love her. I tried to be tough; I never cried or told anybody that my parents were having problems, and nobody knew. I just tried to carry everybody and fix everything. But my dad worked hard at getting me back. And I put him through some terrible things. We never talked much about the divorce; we only mentioned it about four or five times.

JCD: Have you been able to rebuild your relationship?

Girl #12: Yes, through the Lord. He gave me my dad back.

Girl #13: You are making me cry. I have . . . oh, my goodness. I don't cry, because my dad told me never to cry. And . . .

JCD: Your dad was wrong.

Girl #13: I know. He also knows now. He cries all the time. [laughter]

JCD: These personal experiences that you all are sharing are deeply moving. It is obvious that many of you have walked a similar path. You've done well academically, and yet some of you have experienced the same emptiness inside.

Would anyone else like to share your story?

Girl #9: I remember my childhood only vaguely. I recall going fishing with my dad and taking motorcycle rides, but that's about it. When my parents were divorced, my biological dad quit asking me questions about my life. He still doesn't.

I wish he would ask, but he wouldn't care. And so that has scarred me a lot, because I'm hesitant to talk to people about myself. I think what I say really doesn't matter. And I don't know why I'm crying either. I still try to get my dad to do what he ought to do, but I get disappointed every time. [sniffling] I'm just gonna take a breather. [laughter]

My mom and I have been so close, and she will never say anything bad about my dad at all. I admire her a lot for that. [crying] I'm so sorry.

JCD: Please don't apologize. We're dealing with really raw emotions here, and in your case, it is an ache that goes back to when you were very young.

Girl #9: Yeah. I would try to tell my dad some things, but since he wouldn't follow up with it, I'd get disappointed. My mom always warned me about that. She told me not to have expectations for my dad and just let him grow up. And so I've tried. I had lunch with my dad before I came here and told him where I was going. And he just talked about his adopted daughter and what she needs. He totally ignored what I had told him. So I've given up on him. Now I think of him not as a dad but as a "mission field," trying to love him as Christ would, but not as a daughter should.

Girl #15: How often do you see him?

Girl #9: I see him maybe at Christmas and Thanksgiving, times like that. But the good news is that my mom has married a wonderful man who has become a father figure for me. He takes me out on dates often and asks me questions about my life. He never talks about himself. He's made me feel so worthy and tells me how proud he is of me. I've never experienced that before. [weeping] Every time I call my mom, he'll get on the other line too and want to hear. He totally came in and . . . he just cared. He's never missed one of my ball games. My dad never came to any of my games, and that hurt a lot.

So I'm finally getting my confidence back, as though I really do matter.

Girl #16: I don't really have very many memories of my childhood. I remember having my own golf clubs that my father had inscribed for me. So, obviously, we played golf together. I see him regularly now, but he doesn't ask me questions.

When I told him I was going to college, he asked me which one and what I was doing. But that was basically all he said. He didn't want to know why I was going to college or what I wanted to study. He didn't go to college, or as he said, he only "visited" it for a couple of months and then dropped out. He partied and drank too much and left. I basically have lived my life for myself, made all my decisions, and things like that. He's never wanted to help me make decisions.

I have had an interesting relationship with my father. He was very distant when I was young. He didn't know how to communicate at all, which was hard for my mom. That is something I also struggle with, 'cause I don't know how to communicate with people either. My parents were never intimate. I only saw them kiss once in my entire life. So I had no idea what intimacy was or how to express it.

I know my dad loved us, although he never told us he did. You know, we just kind of knew it. Still, I always loved my dad, and I never wanted him to be alone. Then my mom cheated on my dad and that's why they got a divorce. So that's another behavior I learned—cheating and lying about everything.

My mom never told my dad she cheated; she just filed for divorce. So when my parents got divorced, she married the guy she cheated with. My sister decided to live with my mom, and I went with my dad because no one wanted to live with him and I didn't want him to be alone. And we were kind of all rebelling from God. At the time, my dad was the only godly influence in my life. And it was just amazing how he began to open up. He learned how to love me, you know, and show me that he did. Now he's my best friend.

But it took a long time. I did a lot of things to my dad that my mom had done to him. I lied to him and did the other things I had learned at home. But he stood by me. He was definitely there when I needed him. He told me how much he cared about me and how proud he was of me. And today he'll come to me in tears and tell me how much he loves me and that he's so thankful he has a daughter who follows the Lord and listens to Him.

When my dad started showing

me how much he loved me, I realized how much God loves me. I never felt worthy of love by anyone until my dad started showing it to me.

Girl #17: That was true for me. My father came from an abusive home. His dad was an alcoholic, and he was the only Christian out of five brothers. So he purposed in his heart that his family would be different, but at the same time, he's very . . . he's an engineer. He's very mathematical and "equational." For him, A plus B equals C. It is very hard for him to reveal his emotions.

Well, when I was nine years old, I was diagnosed with clinical depression, which was really difficult for my family. There were years of counseling and just battling through it. But during that time, my father stepped outside of himself, and he affirmed me in a very meaningful way. I would apologize for being depressed and say, "Daddy, I don't know what's going on. I can't help it." And he would say, "I love you just the way you are."

You know, that is so huge, and to this day, I know that God has a purpose for my life, because both my dad and my mom affirm me, but my dad did it best. I remember sitting on his lap and hearing him say, "You know, sweetheart, we love you." So I can definitely see how just knowing that has shaped my life. I think it is so important for us as women to hear that we are loved and to be able to feel it. We need to be affirmed—to have a dad say, "You are the apple of my eye" and to let us know it by hugging us.

JCD: Wouldn't it be interesting if the dads you're talking about could have been sitting behind each of you and hearing what you had to say?

Girl #18: I'll bet they'd all be crying too.

JCD: I think you're right.

We would need another box of Kleenex.

Girl #14: Hearing these comments from the other girls makes me realize how blessed I am to have a father who spent time with me when I was growing up. And I'm blown away by what you all are saying. I had no idea of the hurt that so many of you have been through. I'm the second of ten children, which is pretty much a recipe for having a dad who couldn't give me special attention, and yet he spent a lot of time with us individually. He'd get up at five in the morning to take one of us out to breakfast for a couple of hours. He tried to do that with each child once a month. And then when I turned sixteen, he started taking me out to dinner instead. Those were times when he would ask what was going on in my life, and then he would say, "Do you know how proud I am of you? Do you know how much I love you?" Those were the two questions he always asked as we finished eating.

He had another ritual that, even though it was a small thing, meant so much to me. I depended on it every single night. He went around to each of the kids' beds one at a time, and he sat there and scratched our backs and hugged us. And then he said the same prayer over us. He did that throughout our childhoods. It was such a special part of my growing up. I'll tell you, it was very difficult for me when I was away at college not to have him praying for me at bedtime.

JCD: My goodness, what a blessing! What was the prayer your dad said every night?

Girl #14: He would say, "Heavenly Father, thank You for a daughter like Sherrie. Thank You for blessing her and putting her in this family. Thank You for helping her find You at an early age. Protect her tonight as she sleeps and tomorrow as she goes through her day. Keep her from the enemy and from harm. Help her to find a godly husband in Your time. In Jesus' name, amen."

It was always the same, every night.

JCD: Would you allow me to put that prayer in my book?

Girl #14: Yeah, I would love to have you include it.

JCD: That beautiful prayer will be with you for the rest of your life, won't it?

Girl #14: It will. And I'll pray it over my kids too, and I'll encourage my future husband to do it too.

Girl #20: Wow, I didn't realize this was going to be so emotional. Did anyone else come expecting this? We walked in and saw this beautiful luncheon provided for us. I felt like a princess, and then suddenly, here we are all crying. [laughter]

Girl #21: I, too, have been blessed with a father who wanted to be a part of my life. He is a talented man, very athletic; he just has a sense of authority about him. He knows the Word of God inside and out, and that's where he gains his authority. He could have accomplished anything he wanted, but he became an assistant pastor so that he could be with the family.

Then he started his own church and became the head pastor, but he still had time for me. Every week he would say, "Robin, are we gonna have lunch today?" He would actually be bugging me for a date. He would take me on backpacking trips, something that most girls don't get a chance to do because only boys go backpacking. My sister and I would go backpacking in the Sierras with maybe ten dads and their sons. And he made me feel so special because I was worthy of him wanting to be with me. He wanted to hang out with me.

And one more thing. You asked

us for suggestions for dads, and I would like to offer one.

JCD: Please do.

Girl #21: Even though my dad wanted to be with us, sometimes girls have a tendency to be closer to Mom. So when we were little, I mean real little—it started out when maybe I was three or so—we wanted Mom all the time. We wanted Mom to put us to bed; we wanted Mom to wake us up. We wanted Mom to make food. The French toast didn't taste good unless Mom made it. And she began to get worn out, so my dad came up with a little trick. At night my dad made it a priority to put us to bed. Well, at first we didn't want him to do that. So he would say, "Okay, girls, you need to get in bed, close your eyes, and open your mouths. I'm gonna come in there in two minutes, and I have a surprise for you." We never knew what we were going to get. Sometimes it was a little bit of coconut, sometimes it was raisins, but every time my dad would come in and he would put something good in our mouths. We loved it.

JCD: He was bribing you.

Girl #21: Dr. Dobson, it worked. [laughter] We didn't want my mom anymore. [laughter]

But the warmest memory of all for me, and what shaped my life, was waking up very early in the morning and seeing a small light on in another room. It might have been five o'clock or even four. I would get up and find my dad sitting in his chair and holding a cup of coffee. He would be reading the Bible. I would come up beside him and say, "Good morning, Dad." And he would put his arm around me and say, "This is what I just read, Robin. I just prayed this verse for you." And he would put my name beside it in his Bible, and he would pray over me. In fact, right before I came here to the Institute, he prayed for me.

Girl #22: Oh, wow!

JCD: Now you've got to send the Kleenex back down here. [laughter]

Girl #22: That is awesome, Robin.

JCD: Your dad is obviously deeply committed to Christ and to his family, isn't he?

Girl #21: Yeah, he is.

JCD: Well, we are going to have to bring our discussion to a close. This has been a very meaningful and emotional time together, and I deeply appreciate your speaking candidly and from your hearts today. We have used up an entire box of Kleenex, but that is what it was here for.

You are confident and accomplished young women, and yet many of you have revealed a deep "soul hunger" with regard to your fathers. I'm not sure you even knew these things about one another. There has been a common thread here that I didn't anticipate either. I didn't hear great anger or resentment toward your dads—just an ache for affirmation, which many of you never received as a child. You could have talked today about any subject related to *Bringing Up Girls*, but what you have said came from the core of your beings. We have to assume that if you feel the way you do, having come from mostly intact and successful families, millions of other women have dealt with the same unmet need to connect with their dads.

I can't tell you how many women who have read my books or heard my broadcasts have come up to me and said, "You have been the father I never had." I am convinced that few people fully realize just how intense a girl's desire is to connect with the "first man" in her life. If he was absent, or if he is there but not engaged, she will struggle with that vacuum, in some cases for the rest of her life. I will try to convey that message to my readers on your behalf.

Let me conclude by reminding you of what you already know—that there are no perfect mothers and fathers, just as there are no perfect human beings. We are all flawed and selfish and shortsighted at times. Parenting is an enormously difficult task. All of us fail at one point or another. Life itself is extremely demanding, and we all stumble over challenges that we should have handled better. I urge you to forgive those who may have misunderstood the little girl you used to be. Someday you will need to ask for that same forgiving spirit from your grown children.

Second, it is healthy to acknowledge painful experiences from the past, as we have done today. It may even be beneficial in that process to talk to a counselor who can help you come to terms with painful memories. But then you need to release them and move on. One of the most costly mistakes you can make is to harbor bitterness that will damage you from deep inside. You must forgive, which is demanded of us in Scripture, and then you need to let it go. It can be done. It must be done.

Third, I hope you won't confuse your earthly fathers with the love of our heavenly Father. Human beings will fail you at times, but God never rejects, ignores, insults, or disdains His children. He is "a friend who sticks closer than a brother,"[2] and we read in Psalms that He is "close to the brokenhearted."[3] We have heard repeatedly today that some of you have felt estranged from God because your dads failed to affirm you. It is a natural mistake to make because our fathers are often a visual image of the Almighty. Nevertheless, the distinction must not be blurred. God is love. Period!

Fourth and last, a mistake commonly made by those who experienced difficult childhoods is to see themselves as victims who are forever doomed to suffer. With God's help and His healing touch, you can overcome even the most painful obstacles from your early years.

I love the chorus written by Bill and Gloria Gaither some years ago with these lyrics: "Something beautiful, something good. All my confusion, He understood. All I had to offer Him was brokenness and strife, but He made something beautiful of my life."[4]

Thanks again for your openness today. What you have shared will be very helpful to parents. God be with you all.

3

Why Daddies Matter

THE SIGNIFICANCE OF OUR INTERACTION with the Institute students can hardly be overstated. Let me remind you that the women who participated in our discussion were young, intelligent, accomplished, and well educated. It might be said that they "had it all." Nevertheless, they hungered for something more—something inexpressible—that could not be provided by money or social and academic success. As you observed, the majority of the girls spoke of a void inside that was created by the lack of emotional connection with their fathers.

So what was going on there? Was their longing for paternal affirmation and affection unique to the individuals in this group? Certainly not! What the students described is almost universal among girls and women. There is a place in the female soul reserved for Daddy, or a daddy figure, that will always yearn for affirmation. Not every girl or woman is the same, of course, but almost every girl desires a close bond with this most significant man in her life. She will adore him if he loves and protects her and if she finds safety and warmth in his arms. She will feel that way throughout life unless he disappoints her or until one of them dies. She will tend to see all men through the lens of that relationship. If he rejects and ignores her, or worse, if he abuses and abandons her, the yearning within her becomes more intense, though it is often tainted with resentment and anger.

Mothers cannot fill this particular empty space. They can and must meet similar needs for love and adoration, and in fact they do occupy their own real estate in a daughter's heart. A girl without a mother's love is a sad spectacle indeed, and I would not minimize the maternal role in any regard. But moms can't be dads, and dads can't be moms. This is why the current advocacy on behalf of same-sex marriage and homosexual adoption contradicts what is best for children.

Some girls will go to great lengths to achieve a close relationship with their fathers. I am reminded of a man who told me about driving a teenage boy to the home of his thirteen-year-old girlfriend. When they arrived, a pretty little teenybopper popped out of the house dressed like a prostitute. She was wearing fishnet stockings and a shocking see-through dress that revealed just about everything, including her panties and bra. Her father was standing in the front yard when she walked past him. He looked up and said, "Have a nice time."

After the girl was in the car, she explained tearfully that she was wearing the sexy dress because she wanted to see if her dad cared enough to stop her. He didn't. It was just a test of his love and concern. He failed it. When they arrived at their destination, she went into the women's restroom and changed her clothes.

Why do girls and women have such intense needs for affirmation from their fathers, and why does the hurt caused by abandonment or rejection often reverberate for a lifetime? A primary reason for this inner ache is because a daughter's sense of self-worth and confidence is linked directly to her relationship with her dad.[5] What he thinks about her and how he expresses his affection is a central source of her perceived value as a human being. It also affects her femininity and teaches her how to relate to boys and men. Given this vital role in the development of girls, it is a tragedy that 34 percent of these precious babies are born into homes without a father present.[6] They are deprived of fatherly support and influence from the moment of birth!

Counselor and author H. Norman Wright addresses this matter of a woman's sense of identity in his outstanding book *Always Daddy's Girl*. It contains the following cogent observation, written directly for the female reader:

Your relationship with your father was your critical initial interaction with the masculine gender. He was the first man whose attention you wanted to gain. He was the first man you flirted with, the first man to cuddle you and kiss you, the first man to prize you as a very special girl among all other girls. All of these experiences with your father were vital to the nurturing of the element which makes you different from him and all other men: your femininity. The fawning attention of a father for his daughter prepares her for her uniquely feminine role as a girlfriend, fiancée and wife.

If there was something lacking in your relationship with your father when you were a child, the development of your femininity suffered the most. Why? As a little girl, you by nature expressed all the budding traits of the feminine gender. If your father was emotionally or physically absent, or was harsh,

> rejecting or angry toward you, you automatically and subconsciously attached his disapproval to your femininity. You didn't have the intellectual capacity to understand his rejection, nor did you have the inner defensive structure to insulate yourself against it. You simply and naively reasoned, "I want Daddy to like me; Daddy doesn't like me the way I am; I will change the way I am so Daddy will like me."
>
> When a father does not value or respond to his daughter's femininity, she is stunted in her development. When a daughter has little experience in delighting her father as a child, she is incomplete. She is left to discover her femininity for herself, often with tragic results in her relationships with men.[7]

Wright's insightful analysis explains why the young women I quoted in the previous chapter were so emotional about the rejection they felt from their fathers. It tells us why the most casual negative remark made by a dad years ago still echoes in his daughter's heart. It should also say something profound to today's fathers about their own vulnerable little girls.

Please understand that it is not my purpose to browbeat men or disparage their efforts to meet the needs of their children. Most of them are deeply committed to their families and want to be good fathers. Nevertheless, the pace of living and the pressures of work make it difficult to remember what really matters in the grand scheme of things. Former Beatle John Lennon wrote this lyric in one of his final songs: "Life is what happens to you while you're busy making other plans."[8] How little he knew. Lennon had only a few days to live.

Being a father and a type A personality myself, I look back on my parenting experiences and recall instances where I could have done a better job. I wish I could relive some of those busy days at a slower pace. Unfortunately, none of us is allowed do-overs or mulligans. When our record is finally in the books, not a word or a deed can be altered.

Would it be self-serving to tell you that I

also did some things right during my early days as a father, and that the memories of some very special times with my kids rank at the top of my list of accomplishments today? Among my favorites are recollections of my daughter, Danae, when she was five years old. We used to take bike trips together to a nearby park on Saturday mornings. We would play in a sandbox with shovels and buckets. I taught her to build sand castles, explained what a moat and a drawbridge were, and talked about anything else that seemed to interest her. Then we would go to a nearby taco stand and have lunch before riding home. On the way back, we listened every week to a favorite recording of Rodgers and Hammerstein's *Cinderella* on a small Craig recorder, and we sang the songs together. Danae loved those outings, and she can tell you in detail about them today. And guess what? I loved them too.

Our son, Ryan, and I had our fun adventures together too. When he was three years old, I would hide his stuffed bears, lions, deer, and giraffes around the house. Then when it was dark, we'd take my flashlights and his toy guns, and we would creep around on a big game hunt. When he was twelve, we began hunting and fishing together for real. I will never forget those days in the great out-of-doors with my only son. We still hunt together today.

From where I sit today, I can say that nothing, and I mean nothing, from that era turned out to be more significant than the hours I spent with my little family. The relationships we enjoy today were nurtured during those years when it would have been very easy for me to chase every professional prize and ignore what mattered most at home.

What I am trying to convey in this booklet (and in *Bringing Up Girls*) is addressed specifically to dads who are still raising kids and want to respond to the desires of their little hearts. My advice is also relevant to fathers whose daughters are grown. The woman who used to be "Dad's little princess" may still long for what she didn't receive when she was young. Even though these fathers can no longer play in the sandbox with their five-year-olds, it is never too late for them to say, "You are precious to me."

We'll conclude our discussion by offering a few how-to ideas for dads about forging meaningful connections with their daughters. It isn't rocket science, but we all need to be reminded of the obvious every now and then. One of the cornerstones of human relationships is embodied in a single word: *conversation.* Girls and women, more than boys and men, connect emotionally through spoken words. When communication breaks down between them and people they love, females are often wounded and frustrated. Girls often feel abandoned by fathers who won't engage them verbally.

You'll remember that two of the Institute women addressed this issue through their tears. One said that her dad was completely disinterested in who she was or what she was doing. Another said her father "didn't know how to communicate at all," and as a result, she has never understood what intimacy is all about. She never witnessed or experienced it.

Every professional counselor has heard similar personal accounts. Females of all ages tend to interpret masculine silence as evidence of rejection. Based on this understanding, the best thing dads can do to connect with their daughters is to talk to them about whatever is of interest. Ask questions and then listen carefully to what is said in return. This interaction helps to produce the affirmation I have been describing. Meaningful and affectionate dialogue with a daughter is evidence that she is worthy, secure, and loved. Those beneficial effects can be achieved so easily through simple, genuine conversation.

Touch is another point of connection that is essential to girls. Just like their mothers, our daughters need to be hugged regularly, perhaps every day. Hugging is easy to do when girls are young and they see their daddies as champions and best buddies. However, with the arrival of puberty and evidences of sexual maturation, fathers often feel uneasy and tend to avoid physical contact. Girls can read that discomfort with the accuracy of a laser.[9]

During our discussion with the students, one girl gave us a textbook example of the way fathers often respond to their daughters during puberty and adolescence. It is worth repeating:

> When I was going from a child to a woman—experiencing puberty—my dad just totally stepped back from me. It was as though he no longer knew how to relate to me. But it was a time when I desperately needed him in my life.

The awkwardness of this girl's father, I would guess, was related to her breast development and womanly appearance. Some fourteen-or fifteen-year-old girls already have the bodies of women, and their dads are not supposed to notice—but they do. A loving father is afraid he will touch her in the wrong place or otherwise offend her. So he tries to keep a discreet distance.

On the other side of the ledger, a girl who has wrestled with her father and hugged and kissed him throughout childhood can't possibly understand why he leans away now when she throws her arms around him. One commentator called that "the leaning tower of Pisa." There is no way a father can explain what is making him nervous. His attraction to her is involuntary and usually quite innocent. What makes the situation worse is that younger children in the family, both boys and girls, still snuggle up to Dad and tell him they love him. The budding teenager sees that affection and wants to cry over what she has lost.

The Institute student observed her father stepping back from her, and it was natural for her to conclude that "Daddy doesn't love me anymore." That scenario has been enacted by millions of fathers and daughters around the world.

I want to say to all these dads emphatically that your pubescent and adolescent girls are going through a time of great insecurity. They desperately need you now. You are their protector and their source of stability. Your love now is critical to their ability to cope with the rejection, hurt, and fears that are coming at them from their peers. Hugs are needed now more than ever.

I urge fathers to continue providing the

physical contact that was appropriate during earlier childhood. It should not be sexual in nature, of course, but a loving, fatherly response is still vital. The last thing you want to convey now, even inadvertently, is that your love has melted away. So hide the awkwardness, Dad, and hug your kid like you did when she was six!

I received an early lesson on the importance of touch when my son and daughter were three and seven years of age, respectively. Danae has always been very physical with me from her earliest childhood. When I watched a televised football game on a Saturday afternoon, she often climbed on me with her Barbie doll and played on my lap. Then she would move around to my back and climb on my shoulders. When the USC Trojans scored a touchdown, she would giggle and hang on for dear life as I danced around. She was always Daddy's little girl.

But then Danae and Ryan both came down with the chicken pox. Lucky me! I had never had the disease, and I assure you, I didn't want it! Chicken pox can be a nightmare when contracted as a grown adult. Therefore, I scrupulously avoided both my kids for five days. I tried to disguise what I was doing, but my daughter figured it out. Finally, she went crying to her mom and said, "Daddy won't touch me anymore."

That felt like a knife in my heart. It also told me that my daughter still needed physical contact with me. It was one of the ways I affirmed my love for her. As soon as she began to get well, I wrapped my arms around her again. That object lesson was very useful to me later when Danae began to develop. By the way, I didn't come down with the chicken pox and still haven't had it. I'm saving the experience until I am about eighty so everyone will feel sorry for me.

To dads, let me say, "Just keep doin' watcha been doin'." And keep your tower straight! Your daughter will notice if it is leaning.

Here's a final suggestion, another simple idea that is still effective. Dads who want to connect with their little girls, and even those who are not so little, need to spend one-on-one time with them. It is an excellent way to knock down barriers and build bridges. Take your daughter somewhere she will like, such as out to breakfast or dinner. It doesn't have to be a big deal. Just make it a quiet time together when the two of you can sit and talk. Play miniature golf together, or check out a DVD at the library that the two of you can watch at home. If your daughter is younger, go to a kids' movie or a theme park. Put these activities on the calendar, and **do not** let the dates get canceled or postponed. Never leave kids wondering why you didn't show up and didn't even call. That can be more painful to a girl than not promising in the first place.

Once adolescence comes crashing on the scene, your teenager may be embarrassed to be seen with you. That's okay. Play by her rules, whatever they are.

Never forget that girls are made out of the same stuff their mothers are. Put sweet little notes and cards in your daughter's coat pocket or in her shoe. Write a short prayer and put it under her pillow. Girls love flowers. It's in their DNA! They beam when you express pride to others about them. Look for anything that will bring your daughter into your world or you into hers. While you are at it, tell her you love her every time you are together. You will be her hero forever.

I love writing about this subject, because it lies very close to my heart. I'll bet many of you feel the same way.

4

Conclusion

AND SO WE COME to the end of our discussion of dads and daughters. I will end by providing fathers with some practical advice relevant to their daughters.

Remember, Dads

Be the leader of your family by setting boundaries.

Shower your daughter with small gestures of kindness.

Build your daughter up with compliments rather than consistently pointing out her flaws.

Stay connected with your daughter even if you have disappointed or failed her in some way.

Never stop asking your daughter questions about what's going on in her life.

Love your daughter. If she knows her earthly father loves her, it will be easier for her to understand and accept her heavenly Father's love.

Pray with your daughter as often as you can, and when you are away from each other, hold her in your prayers with your wife.

You may notice that there are seven tips above—one for each day in the week. Why not make it your goal this week to try them all? Please do not be discouraged if you are not in the habit of doing some of them. It may feel awkward at first if your daughter shrugs off a compliment or claims she's "too old" for a hug. I assure you that in her heart, she will notice that you are reaching out to her. We know from previous pages how much that means to a girl. Keep looking for opportunities to demonstrate your love and commitment. With God's help, you will recognize them. May He bless this precious daughter He has loaned to you for a brief season.

Notes

1. See http://www.focusleadership.org.
2. Proverbs 18:24
3. Psalm 34:18
4. William J. Gaither and Gloria Gaither, "Something Beautiful" (copyright 1980).
5. Tanya S. Scheffler and Peter J. Naus, "The Relationship between Fatherly Affirmation and a Woman's Self-Esteem, Fear of Intimacy, Comfort with Womanhood and Comfort with Sexuality," *Canadian Journal of Human Sexuality* 8, no. 1 (Spring 1999): 39-45; Margaret J. Meeker, *Strong Fathers, Strong Daughters: 10 Secrets Every Father Should Know* (Washington, D.C.: Regnery Publishing, 2008).
6. National Vital Statistics, Volume 52, no. 10, 2002. See http://www.cdc.gov/nchs/data/nvsr/nvsr52/nvsr52_10.pdf.
7. H. Norman Wright, *Always Daddy's Girl* (Ventura, CA: Regal, 2001), 35-36.

8. John Lennon, "Beautiful Boy" (1980). Versions of this same quote have been attributed to several individuals over the years, including Betty Talmadge, Thomas LaMance, Margaret Millar, Lily Tomlin, William Gaddis, and Allen Saunders.
9. Meeker, *Strong Fathers, Strong Daughters*, 96; Debra Haffner, *Beyond the Big Talk: A Parent's Guide to Raising Sexually Healthy Teens—from Middle School to High School and Beyond* (New York: Newmarket Press, 2001).

Tune in to
Family Talk with Dr. James Dobson.

To learn more about
Family Talk with Dr. James Dobson
or to find a station in your area,
visit http://www.myfamilytalk.com
or call (877) 732-6825.